When the Mountain Doesn't Move

5 Weeks of Choosing Faith

Carrie Zeilstra

When the Mountain Doesn't Move: 5 Weeks of Choosing Faith

Dear Friend,

I have been praying that these words would reach you. God placed you on my heart as I typed each letter. I pray that God draws you closer to him through this 5-week journey. (Although, you have permission to take as many days as you need! Sometimes the Holy Spirit may want you to sit with one lesson before you move on to the next. And other times you may just get off schedule. No judgment here, Friend. Just pick up where you left off and press on.)

Each day has a reflection section called "Finding Your Footing." I encourage you to write your reflections in the spaces provided - even if that's not your "thing." We don't always get to see what God is doing in real time. However, when we record what God is teaching us, it allows us to look back and see his hand at work.

It may be a challenging climb, but let's journey together toward choosing faith, even when the mountain doesn't move.

Blessings,

Carrie

Contents

When the Mountain Doesn't Move

Week One

When the Mountain Doesn't Move

"'For truly, I say to you, if you have faith like a grain of mustard seed, you will say to this mountain, 'Move from here to there,' and it will move, and nothing will be impossible for you.'"
Matthew 17:20

The number of the fertility specialist flashed across the screen of my ringing phone. I grabbed it and ran to my room for a little privacy.

This is it! I thought, ready to celebrate the good news I was about to receive.

"Hello?" I answered breathlessly.

"Mrs. Zeilstra?"

"Yes?" My heart pounded. I sat on the edge of my bed and tried to focus.

"We received the results of your blood test." The kind-sounding voice paused. "Unfortunately, the results show that you are not pregnant."

I hung up the phone seconds later. Tears filled my eyes as I slid from the edge of the bed to the floor.

"I was so sure, Father." I whispered my prayer as I cried. "We prayed. We pleaded. You gave us hope. You gave us peace as we waited. I thought you were moving mountains for us. We were trusting you to move mountains."

God chose not to move the mountain of infertility for me and my husband. The phone call that day came after the last infertility treatment we were willing to try.

It was our last-ditch effort after years of infertility, a long adoption process that resulted in a dead end, and the death of our infant daughter. My husband and I simply wanted to give our son a living sibling. But after 6 years of prayer, loss, grief, and disappointment we still were unable to add to our family.

My heart was filled with painful questions. I wondered why God wasn't moving mountains for me and my family. Why wasn't he rescuing us from the pain? Why wasn't he giving me what my heart longed for? Why did he give us hope just to take it away?

When the things we pray against are the very things God allows, we are left with insurmountable questions. Sometimes God chooses not to move the mountain before us. In those times Matthew 17:20 can feel like a lie.

When the dust settles, we stand at the base of the mountain that we expected to move, full of uncertainty and with no small amount of hurt in our hearts.

If you are currently in that place, there are no easy

explanations. There are no magic words I can type to make the pain disappear.

After that heartbreaking phone call, we had exhausted every option. We prayed for miracles. But the mountain of loss, grief, and disappointment remained.

Even so, I now see how God did in fact use my faith to move mountains in that season. **He moved mountains of doubt, mountains of whys, and mountains of pain,** all because of my decision to choose faith in him, no matter how I felt.

What if we choose faith? Faith - even if the mountain we told to move, still stands firmly in place. Faith that God remains with us and will help us with the difficult climb ahead. And **faith that he is moving mountains, even if they are not the ones we expected to move.**

With faith "nothing will be impossible for you" (Matthew 17:20). Even when the mountain ahead doesn't move.

Dear Heavenly Father,
You know my heart.
You know my hurts and disappointments.
I have prayed for circumstances to change
and yet they have not. I know you alone
are in control. Please show me your
presence as you help me through this
situation that seems impossible. Move the
mountains of my doubts as I seek you.
In Jesus' Name, Amen

Finding Your Footing

Is there a mountain in your life that seems unmoving, even after countless prayers of faith? If so, what questions and disappointments are you wrestling with because of that circumstance?

____

____

____

____

Read all of Hebrews chapter 11. Note verses 39-40. Did those commended for their faith in this chapter have hardship removed from their lives? What do you know about the individuals listed in this chapter?

____

____

____

____

Extra Notes

When Your Soul is Weary

"Come to me, all who labor and are heavy laden, and I will give you rest. Take my yoke upon you, and learn from me, for I am gentle and lowly in heart, and you will find rest for your souls. For my yoke is easy, and my burden is light."
Matthew 11:28-30

Several years ago, my husband and I entered something called an "Adventure Race." It was one of those "let's try something new together" experiences that we were both looking forward to.

We were both fairly active and competitive people. We were excited for the challenge! But we were nowhere *near* prepared for what we faced that day. I can't be sure of the number of miles we covered, but it was six solid hours of moving forward. Running, hiking, biking, and even paddle boarding.

"We're almost there," I told my body on the last leg of the race. We were hiking over seemingly endless sand dunes along Lake Michigan.

"When we get to the top of this one, we'll be able to see the end." My husband said between breaths. He strode ahead of me, reaching the peak first.

Normally I would try to keep up, but my competitive spirit disappeared somewhere in the sand. I watched my husband's shoulders slump. And when I caught up with him a few seconds later, I saw why.

We squinted in the direction of the finish line. But all that we could see was more sand. Peak after peak of sand.

The weariness threatened to win. I was no longer worried about what our time would be when we crossed the finish line. I was just praying my tired bones could make it to our car.

My husband and I kept encouraging each other to "just keep moving." We finally did make it to the finish and our nearby car. But I am not too proud to admit that I crawled down the last sand dune.

Needless to say, our first adventure race was also our last. I have never felt that sort of physical exhaustion and hope to avoid ever feeling that way again!

Many of us know that type of mental, emotional, or spiritual exhaustion. We know what it's like to think we are almost to the other side of the mountain, just to realize we are nowhere near finished with the journey. Peak after peak of hardships stretch out as far as we can see.

When we experience difficult times, there is social pressure to "just keep moving." We may even chide ourselves for not being able to handle it all.

But God doesn't dismiss our worn souls. Instead, He promises us rest.

Our key verse for today is spoken by Jesus himself. It was likely a countercultural statement at the time, and it still is today.

Jesus doesn't say to "pick yourself up and move on." He doesn't praise the heavy burdened for the weight they carry. He doesn't even offer to simply cheer the weary ones on as they push forward.

No, **Jesus validates our exhausted state and desires to help us.**

Rather than coaching us toward a finish line that the world has set, Jesus invites us to simply go to him. "Come to me…"

Then, instead of offering us success by the world's standards, Jesus offers something that only he can – *rest*. Rest for our souls in the middle of hardship and a burden that is light.

When life weighs us down with burdens and the hardships ahead seem unending, Jesus wants to ease our journey. As we experience seasons of soul weariness, may we find rest for our spirits as we draw near to Jesus.

*Dear Heavenly Father,
You alone can bring rest to my
weary soul. Lord, show me your mercy by
lifting my heavy burdens. Grant me peace
and rest that can only come from you.
In Jesus' Name, Amen*

Finding Your Footing

Read Exodus 33:14. What does God promise Moses? Can we, as believers in Christ, expect the same promise?

____

____

____

____

What is your heavy burden in this season of life? Is it one stressor or multiple? Write out a prayer using the phrases from Matthew 11:28-30 to lay your burdens at the feet of Jesus.

____

____

____

____

____

Extra Notes

When God Says No

"And going a little farther he fell on his face and prayed, saying, "My Father, if it be possible, let this cup pass from me; nevertheless, not as I will, but as you will." Matthew 26:39

The story of Jesus in the Garden of Gethsemane is a beautiful yet heartbreaking glimpse into his humanity. Although I will never know that kind of anguish, I can relate to Christ in those moments.

That night in the darkness of the garden, Jesus felt troubled. He felt let down and betrayed by those who were closest to him. Jesus said, "My soul is very sorrowful, even to death" (Matthew 26:38).

Perhaps what I can relate to most is Jesus's desperate prayer to avoid the pain he knew was coming.

How often do we do the same?

Nothing brings me to the point of knee-callusing prayer like when I am asking God to deliver me or someone I love from suffering. I know I am not the only one. We pray hard when we are headed into a difficult situation. We too can feel so overwhelmed by sorrow that all we can do is fall to our knees and pray for circumstances to change.

This isn't something to be ashamed of. There are examples throughout the Bible of faithful followers doing the same.

In our key verse today, we see Jesus himself pleading with God in the garden of Gethsemane. We know that Jesus spent significant time with his father in prayer throughout his ministry. But this is the only time recorded in the Bible we see Jesus pleading with God to avoid hardship.

Jesus knew the pain he was about to suffer. We read that Jesus fell to his face, and he pleaded with his father for another way.

Yet, in the next breath Jesus submitted to his father's will. (Matthew 27:39)

God, all-knowing, compassionate, yet just, knew there was no other way. So, despite Jesus's agony, God said "No" to his only son's plea. God did not allow the cup of pain to pass from Jesus. God said "yes" to his own will. **Not because he didn't love Jesus enough to spare him from the pain of death, but because he loved *us* so much, he desired eternity with us.**

None of us are going through what Jesus went through in the garden that night. My guess is that most of us have never been in such agony that we sweat blood (Luke 22:44). Not one of us has carried the weight of the sins of the world on our shoulders.

However, we *do* know what it's like to cry out to our heavenly father in despair, just as Jesus did that night in the garden.

Most of us know what it's like when God says "no" to our most anguished requests. So did Jesus.

Some believe that a "no" from God, always means a lack of faith. My friend, that is simply not true. Our perfect Savior, Christ Jesus himself, received a "no" from God.

When God says "no," it does not mean our faith in him is lacking. Our faith is what sustains us, even when God says "no." Our faith is what helps us survive the pain which God allows, trusting that he will do something bigger than we can see on this side of the mountain of despair.

Christ demonstrated that we can be brave enough to ask God to spare us from pain. And, because of our faith, we can also have the courage to submit to our heavenly father's will. Even if his will means we experience pain. **What if we learn to follow Christ's example and sacrifice our comfort, for God's will? What if we could trust that our pain is not the end of the story?**

God loves us enough to see his only son suffer on the cross for our sins. When we choose faith in his love for us, we can follow Christ's example and pray - *"Not as I will, but as you will."*

Dear Heavenly Father,
Thank you for loving me enough
to give your son, Jesus, so I can have
eternity with you. Thank you for giving me
hope beyond this life. Your will is difficult to
understand in this season. But I will trust in
your love. Lord, not as I will but as you will.
In Jesus's Name, Amen

Finding Your Footing

Read the entire account of Jesus on the night before his death in Luke 22:39-45 and Matthew 26:36-46. Write down at least one way you relate to Jesus's humanity in those moments.

____

____

____

____

Write about a time in your life that God said 'no' to a desperate prayer. Read Hebrews 5:7-9. What hope can we cling to because of Jesus's obedience?

____

____

____

____

____

____

Extra Notes

When You Are Wounded

"He heals the brokenhearted and binds up their wounds." Psalms 147:3

"Ouch!" I yelped, instinctively pulling my hand toward my chest. The knife I had been cleaning dropped into the sink. I was afraid to look at my finger. All the worst-case scenarios ran through my head as I looked around my empty house.

Oh this is bad! Will I need stitches? Will I be able to drive myself to the hospital?

I prepared for the worst as I opened my clenched fist over the sink. To my surprise the wound didn't seem too bad.

It's probably deeper than it looks. I told myself, but I was unwilling to examine it much closer. *It probably will take a while to heal. And this part of my hand will get easily infected.*

For days I fussed over my finger like it was my job. I was just certain it wasn't going to heal correctly.

Less than one week after my knife cleaning accident, I realized there wasn't even a scab on my finger. I wondered how such an injury could be completely

completely healed already.

You were made to heal.

I gasped. Recognizing that this wasn't a random thought that just jumped into my head. It was the still small voice of the Holy Spirit.

I made you to heal.

Tears filled my eyes. I knew God wasn't talking to me about my finger. He was speaking to me about my heart.

The word "healing" had come up several times in my weekly therapy sessions. And I openly admitted I didn't think it was possible for my heart to heal from some of its deepest wounds.

That day God reminded me that he created my body with the capacity to heal. And as amazing as that cellular process is, he doesn't want to stop there.

Our creator knows our deepest wounds. Not just the physical ones. But the wounds that affect our very souls.

Wounds caused by hurtful words. Broken promises. Whispered gossip. Trauma. Abuse. Grief. Loss. The wrongs done to us by others. Or the haunting guilt of our own actions. We carry these wounds in our souls. We allow them to define us.

But God desires better for us. **He says we are worth saving. We are worth healing.**

Our Heavenly Father made our souls with the capacity to heal. Not only that, but he wants to be the very one who heals us!

Sometimes we resist healing. Perhaps we believe that healing isn't possible for such deep wounds. Or maybe that healing means the hurt wasn't significant.

However, God doesn't expect us to be unchanged by the pain we experience. In fact, he desires to bring redeeming change through our wounds.

(Remember - Christ himself bore the scars from the cross in his resurrected body. Demonstrating to us that pain leaves a mark.)

Just like my finger, it takes time and care to heal our souls. Can you picture God carefully wrapping your heart in a bandage? That is the kind of father we have! He cares about our hurts.

Binding up our wounds doesn't instantly heal them. It's a process. One that takes our cooperation as we allow God to work. But we can step into that process knowing that the God who heals (Exodus 15:26) cares deeply for our hearts and souls.

Praise God that he can use even scars to tell of his redemption and healing!

Dear Heavenly Father,
I praise you, for you are the
God who heals (Exodus 15:26).
Soften my heart to receive your healing.
Bind up my broken heart like only you can.
Show me how to trust you
with my deepest wounds.
In Jesus' Name, Amen

Finding Your Footing

Read 1 Peter 2:24. Contemplate how Christ's wounds bring healing for us.

____

____

____

____

Are you resisting healing in an area of your life? If so, write out a prayer using today's key verse and ask God for his help.

____

____

____

____

____

Extra Notes

When The Earth Gives Way

"God is our refuge and strength, a very present help in trouble. Therefore we will not fear though the earth gives way, though the mountains be moved into the heart of the sea." Psalm 46:1-2

On March 13th, 2020, I made a casual trip to my favorite store. There was an unusually long line. People in front of me all had carts loaded with food, entertainment, and toilet paper. So much toilet paper!

Of course, I had heard of the Coronavirus on the news and a little about how it had affected other countries. But I couldn't imagine it was going to be as bad as the rumors indicated it would.

So there I stood with my sparse-looking red cart, wondering if I too should leave my spot to go get toilet paper. When I finally made it to the front of the line, the cashier asked what I would do if the world shut down.

Naively, I chuckled and said "I love being home! Sounds like the perfect excuse to stay in my PJs and watch movies!"

I didn't think this sounded too bad. It would be like the

year before when snowstorms kept us from leaving the house for a week.

Oh, how wrong I was.

Weeks later, the virus was spreading and taking the lives of many, including several people we knew.

In addition, my job abruptly halted, grocery stores seemed bare, and tension grew inside our house. (There is nothing like being stuck at home with an angsty pre-teen and a husband trying to figure out big work problems from our guest bedroom-turned-office.)

I'm sure you have your own story of difficulty in the unprecedented experience that was 2020 and beyond. For most of us the world as we knew it crumbled. The structure of our routines changed immediately. We experienced losses we never expected. And nothing seemed certain.

For me (like many others), 2020 marked the beginning of a downward spiral of my mental health. Depression and anxiety began to alter my life in more ways than the pandemic ever could. One afternoon, I sat on the couch and cried out to God. He brought a verse to mind. I grabbed a pen and wrote the scripture on my arm.

"God is our refuge and strength, a very present help in trouble." Psalm 46:1

I needed to literally wear this word from the Lord because I was so overwhelmed. It felt like anxiety had taken up permanent residence in my body.

This verse didn't immediately fix my circumstances. I didn't know it at the time, but my mental illness was already present, the isolation of the pandemic just took away my healthy and unhealthy coping mechanisms.

Thankfully, I found sanctuary in the safe place of the Lord. Even in the darkest days of depression, he was my very present help. I didn't trust my own thoughts, but I knew I could trust him. Looking back, I can see God's presence and strength helped me survive that season.

When we experience the world as we know it crumbling beneath us, God's presence can be our lifeline. He desires to be our refuge, strength and help. In the middle of a broken world that we struggle to understand, the Lord is constant. We can count on his word to bring truth. **We can find strength to survive even when our worlds are turned upside down.**

Hardship takes many different forms. The mountain you are climbing may be one of mental or physical illness, loss, disappointment, or unmet expectations. No matter what type of hardship you are facing, God wants to be your refuge. He wants to be your safe place to run for strength and help.

Dear Heavenly Father,
I praise you for being my
refuge when it feels like the world
is falling apart around me.
You are the constant in an ever-changing
world. Show me how to depend on you for
strength and help.
In Jesus' Name, Amen

Finding Your Footing

Look up the definition of "refuge." Write the definition that closest fits the way it is used in Psalm 46:1-2.

____

____

____

____

Read Psalm 91. Choose one verse from this chapter to write out as a prayer to the Lord when trouble comes.

____

____

____

____

____

Extra Notes

When the Mountain Doesn't Move

Week Two

When You Need to Hear the Truth

"Return to your rest, my soul, for the Lord has been good to you." Psalms 116:7 NIV

I swiftly made my way around the spring floor toward a wide-eyed gymnast in a sparkly leotard. I have coached competitive gymnastics for over 15 years. I love the challenge, excitement, and mental toughness gymnastics requires. I coach young ladies with mountains of determination and minds of warriors.

I could tell this wide-eyed warrior was nervous by the way she picked her nails and chewed her lip. She made eye contact with me as I neared.

"Just breathe," I mouthed. Then I took an exaggerated breath in and out. She copied my motions.

Finally, I stood before my gymnast. I had known her long enough to understand that the hardest challenge for her was not the tumbling she was about to perform in her floor routine, but the thoughts of self-doubt racing through her mind.

"Let's hear it!" I smiled. She knew what this meant.

She dropped her hands to her side and repeated the phrase we rehearsed many times.

"I've done it before; I can do it again." She said softly. "But what if…"

"Nope." I interrupted. "We're not letting our minds go there. Tell me again."

She feigned annoyance, then smiled. "I've done it before; I can do it again." She confidently.

A few seconds later the judge called the sparkly warrior's name and she walked onto the floor with confidence. In my coaching career, I teach gymnasts to preach to themselves.

"Tell yourself what you want to believe… even if you're unsure. Your mind will follow."

Guess what? It works!

I know this. I've seen the results on the competition floor. Yet, I often forget this when it comes to my spiritual life.

When difficulties arise, I frequently let my mind spiral. I think of all the worst-case scenarios. I replay the hurt. I tell myself I can't take another step. Somehow, I find a way to both wallow in helplessness and act like it is up to me to fix everything.

Many of the psalmists seemed to understand this concept of "preaching" to themselves. We see this in Psalm 23 (perhaps one of the most well-known Psalms). David penned –

"The Lord is my shepherd; I shall not want. He makes me lie down in green pastures. He leads me beside still waters. He restores my soul. He leads me in paths of righteousness for his name's sake." Psalm 23:1-3

We don't know the circumstances surrounding David when he wrote these words, but we *do* know that he went through several seasons of hardships. **David wrote the words he needed to hear. He used his words to will his heart toward the Lord as he stepped forward in the valley.**

Today's key verse has been an encouragement to me when I find myself in the valley. When I say Psalm 116:6 aloud, I encourage my soul to "rest" from anxiety and remind myself of the goodness the Lord has shown to me in the past.

The truth is God's word is far more powerful than any mantra we come up with ourselves! Because "the unfolding of [his] words gives light" Psalm 119:30. God's word brings the light of peace, courage, and clarity. The truth of scripture gives our thoughts an anchor to hold on to when everything seems uncertain. **We can arm ourselves with short "self-sermons" from God's word that infuse us with the confidence we need for the moment.**

When we face spiraling thoughts, we can preach to our souls. Because of God's faithfulness, we can say with confidence *"HE has done it before, and HE will do it again."*

Dear Heavenly Father,
You are faithful and your
word is true. I am facing a mountain
of uncertainty. Help me choose to anchor my
thoughts on your truth, instead of on my
feelings. Give rest to my soul as I trust in
your goodness.
In Jesus' Name, Amen

Finding Your Footing

Read Psalm 116:1-13. What statements did the psalmist say in the past that were focused on his struggles (verses 10-11)? When he focuses on the Lord, what statements show he is "preaching" truth to himself? (Hint - there are several!)

____

____

____

____

Write out 3-5 verses that encourage your heart in this season. Commit to reading through them, out-loud if possible, once a day for the rest of our study. (Feel free to use a few of my favorites - Psalm 13:5-6, Psalm 27:13, Exodus 14:14, Proverbs 23:18, and today's key verse Psalm 116:7)

____

____

____

____

Extra Notes

When You Can't See the Light

"Finally, brothers, whatever is true, whatever is honorable, whatever is just, whatever is pure, whatever is lovely, whatever is commendable, if there is any excellence, if there is anything worthy of praise, think about these things." Philippians 4:8

I stood in awe, looking up at a plant that I imagined to be as tall as Jack's bean stalk. At the top of the tall stem, I could see what looked like a giant flower.

It looks strong enough to climb! I thought.

Before I could test my theory, my grandma called out from another part of her garden. "That's a sunflower."

"Why is it so big?" I asked, stepping back, knowing grandma would not approve of me climbing her bean stalk... or sunflower.

Grandma laughed. "They grow tall, don't they." She walked toward me, smiling.

"What I like best about sunflowers, is they are always smiling at the sun." She pointed up to the giant flower. "You see, the face of the sunflower moves as the sun moves."

I furrowed my brow and strained on my tiptoes to see the "face" my grandma was talking about. My 5-year-old mind pictured a smiley face in the middle of the bright yellow pedals.

(Admittedly, it took far longer than it should have for me to realize that sunflowers do not have two eyes, a nose, and a smile, as I imagined.)

I've often thought that I want to be like a growing sunflower. Drinking up every ounce of the goodness from the Lord. Desperate to catch every ray of light.

Paul instructs us in Philippians 4:8 to think about things that are *honorable, just, pure, lovely, commendable, excellent, and worthy of praise.*

Each of these are qualities of our God. **Paul is urging us to be drawn to things that reflect God's character. Continuing to set our minds on these things helps us grow in the knowledge of him.** Just as the smiling sunflower grows as it sets its "face" to follow the sun.

But what do we do in times of darkness? When our circumstances seem a world away from excellent or lovely?

Paul's instructions in Philippians 4 didn't come from a sunny, happy place. No, Paul penned these words from the darkness of a prison cell. He knew what it was like to have to recall God's goodness when it was difficult to see.

Recently, I learned something new about the "smiley" sunflower. Once a sunflower's strong, soaring stalk has completed its growth, the flower stays facing east, no longer moving with the sun. The sunflower positions itself to catch the sunlight each morning. Its stalk is sturdy enough to stand tall, even when the sun is behind it.

It is *faith* that holds us steady and strong, just like the sunflower stalk, when the sun is nowhere in our sight. **Faith stands ready, waiting for the sun to rise. Because faith *knows* that even when the night seems unending, the light will appear again.**

There may be seasons of life, when we can see evidence of God's goodness all around us. Other seasons, we may feel stuck waiting for the night to end. In these dark seasons, it can be difficult to see God's goodness.

When we experience circumstances that threaten to knock us down, we can find strength in our faith in God. We can recall what we know about his character – he is *honorable, just, pure, lovely, commendable, excellent, and worthy of praise.*

We can stand firm in our knowledge of him, even as we wait for the night to end.

Dear Heavenly Father,
You are honorable. You are just.
You are lovely, commendable, and
excellent. You are worthy of all my praise.
I choose faith in who you are, even when my
circumstances make it hard to see you.
Strengthen my faith in your goodness. Help
me to see ways in which you are working.
In Jesus' Name, Amen

Finding Your Footing

Choose one thing from Philippians 4:8 to "think on."
Write down the phrase "God is (the word you chose)."
Then write 3 examples that support that statement from
your own life. or scripture.

____

____

____

____

____

Read Numbers 6:24-26. Write this blessing out as a
personalized prayer for your life.

____

____

____

____

Extra Notes

When the Ceiling is Silent

"I love the Lord because he has heard my voice and my pleas for mercy. Because he inclined his ear to me, therefore I will call on him as long as I live."
Psalm 116:1-2

"Sometimes, when I pray to God, it feels like I'm just talking to the ceiling. But I just keep talking to him."

I stared back at the older woman who spoke these words at a bible study group. Astonished by her honesty.

Me too, girl! I wanted to shout. But I held my tongue in favor of a more appropriate conversation after our group time wrapped up.

I'm sure if we're honest, we could all relate to her statement. We pray and wonder if God is even listening. We don't usually see him move right away.

Maybe like me, you have stared at the ceiling, fought to focus, and wondered if you were crazy to think that the God of all creation is listening to your feeble prayer.

In times of desperation, I expect God to somehow show me that he is listening. Yet often I pour out my heart to him and I don't *feel* any different. Silence answers back. My circumstances haven't immediately changed.

In those moments I can't help but wonder if God is even listening.

We can find courage in this – **God's word says that he hears us!** He hears our cries and our desperation. He hears our requests and our praises.

He may not show up in a bright flash of light, or an instant *feeling* of change. Sometimes we may not even *feel* peace after prayer. Even so, we can trust that God is listening! He cares for us (1 Peter 5:7).

Prayer is an act of faith. Faith that when we call out to our Heavenly Father, he hears us. We choose to have faith that the Lord turns his ear toward us.

The author of Psalm 116 does *not* say, 'I love the Lord for he fixed all my problems.' *No!* He says, **"I love the Lord, for he heard my voice." (v. 1)**

Could it be enough to know that God is listening?

Could we commit calling out to him, simply because we trust that he hears us?

When we pray, we should not expect a supernatural feeling, or instant delivery. (Although there are times God will work that way.)

We call on him because we long to be *heard* by God

who holds all things (Colossians 1:17). Through our prayers, we find his mercy in our desperation.

Just keep talking to him, as my honest bible study friend said.

Even when the ceiling is silent, we can keep calling out to him. Again, and again - as long as we live.

Dear Heavenly Father,
Thank you for turning your ear
to me. I trust that you hear me at this very
moment. I confess that sometimes I expect
you to respond right away.
Help me find peace in the knowledge that
you have heard each of my cries.
In Jesus' Name, Amen

Finding Your Footing

Read Psalm 18:6, Psalm 40:1, and Psalm 66:19-20. What encouragement do you find in these verses?

____

____

____

____

Think of a time when God worked in a circumstance after you prayed, even if you didn't recognize it at the time. Write down what you learned about God during that time.

____

____

____

____

____

Extra Notes

When You Face the Unexpected

"When you pass through the waters, I will be with you; and through the rivers, they shall not overwhelm you; when you walk through fire you shall not be burned, and the flame shall not consume you." Isaiah 43:2

I may not have admitted it out loud, but there was a time I assumed that if I was good enough, God would give me a good life. I believed that if I obeyed his commandments and tried to be loving toward others, God would keep me from difficulties, and would give me the life I dreamed of.

How false this belief was. God doesn't promise a trouble-free life.

Throughout scripture, we see that God does not keep those he loves from suffering. In fact, it seems that those who God uses in big ways also suffer in big ways. Job, Joseph, Moses, Daniel, David, and even Jesus's disciples, just to name a few. They were all faithful and obedient followers of God. Yet, they endured the suffering of loss, betrayal, prison, a lion's den, a desert, war, and persecution. Our perfect Savior experienced hardship in his life, even before the cross.

Today's key verse is a beautiful reminder of the promise that God *does* make. In this passage, the Lord says *when* (not if) we walk through hardships, *he will be with us.*

God doesn't promise he will make our path easy, or even the path we planned. But God promises his *presence.* Life on this side of eternity is marred by sin. With sin comes pain, death, brokenness, and suffering.

Jesus says, *"In this world you will have trouble"* (John 16:33a). Our Savior doesn't want us to be surprised by this fact. He knew what it was like to live in this world.

Jesus himself experienced physical pain, loss, overwhelming sorrow, betrayal, and exhaustion. Jesus was fully human and can sympathize with our human experience (Hebrews 4:15).

But there is good news! Jesus goes on to say "But take heart! I have overcome the world" (John 16:33b). What does Jesus mean when he says these words? **Jesus, the perfect son of God, overcame death so we can have the hope of eternity with him.**

We will experience hard times on this side of eternity. But God promises us that he is with us in the hard times. And because of Christ, our hard times will not last forever. When we trust that he died for our sins and rose from the dead to show that he has conquered sin and death, we have hope beyond this life.

We share in Christ's victory, and for now, we must also share in his suffering (Romans 8:17).

When we go through deep waters, God promises not to abandon us. He will not let us be swept away. When we put our faith in his salvation, he will rescue us from eternal suffering.

Let us cling to the promise of his presence in each step of our difficult journey as we look forward to the hope of eternity.

Dear Heavenly Father,
I know you have not promised
an easy journey through this life.
I trust that you are with me. Allow your
presence to sustain me.
I praise you, for you have overcome the
troubles of this world through Christ.
Continue to strengthen my understanding of
your promises.
In Jesus' Name, Amen

Finding Your Footing

Read Isaiah 43:1-2. Write down what you learn about God in these verses.

Do you have any false beliefs or unspoken expectations of God that you may be holding on to? Ask God to reveal through his word what is true, because his word is truth (John 17:17).

Extra Notes

When Questions Outnumber Answers

"The Lord is good, a stronghold in the day of trouble: he knows those who take refuge in him."
Nahum 1:7

"I don't understand how a good God would allow babies to die," I sobbed.

It had been nearly a year since we said goodbye to our daughter, Faith Isabella. I had just started to believe that I might just survive the heaviness of grief.

But then, I heard the devastating news that a friend's 9-month-old baby girl had just died. My friend and I were pregnant at the same time. We were supposed to be planning play dates together, not grieving the loss of our daughters together. The unfairness crushed my already shattered heart.

I wrestled with God for months. Honestly, I was ready to turn away from him, because of all of my unanswered questions.

Several months after her daughter passed, my friend and I attended an event for grieving mothers. I went to support my friend, but my own heart was hardened with anger at the time.

One of the speakers stood before the crowd, looking into the eyes of women who had been through the unimaginable. She held a Bible in one hand and a microphone in the other. I wanted to shut out her words, but then she said something that shook me.

"There is nothing good about the death of your child." She paused to collect herself and I tried not to gasp.

That doesn't sound right, I thought.

"There is nothing good about that loss, it is only bad," she continued. "But God is good. God is the creator of all good. And he can create something good out of that which is only bad."

I don't remember much else from that night. But those words rang in my head for days.

Could this be true, God? I prayed. Is it okay to simply recognize that losing Faith Isabella is bad while also believing that you are good?

Previously, I thought God expected me to declare that the death of our baby girl was good, simply because he is good. I thought he wanted me to deny my grief in order to show my belief that he is working all things together for my good.

My thoughts were far from the truth!

Throughout the Bible, we see examples of bad circumstances in contrast to our good God. In fact, the entirety of God's word is the story of glorious redemption for a world badly corrupted by sin.

So how can a good God allow such bad things?

This is a question that many wrestle with. Many choose to turn away from God because they cannot find an answer to this question that satisfies their hurting heart. I almost made that same choice.

The truth is - circumstances can be only bad. But the Lord is only good. It takes faith to believe that *both* could be true at the same time. And we must remember that faith is a choice that is not based on our feelings.

Faith stands in the midst of bad and claims that God is good (Psalm 145:9). Faith stands in the darkest night and claims that the Lord is their light (Micah 7:8). Faith doesn't demand an explanation from the Lord, but instead seeks refuge and strength in him (Psalm 46:1).

God is good. He is the creator of all good. Only God can perform the miracle of creating good out of something bad.

When we choose faith in the Lord, we choose to be a part of that miracle, and a part of his good plans and purposes.

Dear Heavenly Father,
I praise you for being a good God.
I know that you are good,
even when I am surrounded by bad
circumstances. Help me to take refuge in
you. Help me see evidence of your goodness,
even in the middle of difficult times.
In Jesus' Name, Amen

Finding Your Footing

Read Psalm 145:8-9. What do you learn about God's character in these verses? Is he angry when we wrestle with hard questions?

____

____

____

____

Lament is a part of faith in hardship. God wants us to come to him with our hurts. Read Psalm 6 (a psalm of lament). Write out the verses you can most relate to.

____

____

____

____

Extra Notes

When the Mountain Doesn't Move

Week Three

When Choas Captures Your Mind

*"You keep him in perfect peace whose mind is stayed
on you because he trusts in you. Trust in the Lord
forever, for the Lord God is an everlasting rock."*
Isaiah 26:3-4

Whenever I see a pinball machine, I can't help but
play. But boy, am I bad at it! Without fail, I launch the
ball into the flashing lights and shapes that bump it
around. Then, I feverishly start poking the buttons to
try to keep the ball from falling.

Bing, Bing, Bing... The noise from the game adds to the
chaos.

I keep erratically stabbing the buttons because it gives
me the illusion that I have some control over that
stinking metal ball. But I'm never patient enough to
actually figure out what each button does, or how to
time my attack.

Inevitably, the metal ball falls into the abyss. Yet, I
waste no time launching the next ball and starting the
whole thing over again. When my time is up, I have
accomplished nothing, and my far-too-competitive
spirit is left wishing for my quarters back. But the next
time I see a pinball machine, I'll do it all over again.

Sometimes my thought life is similar to my pinball strategy.

My mind bounces from one thing to another. Planning, worrying, obsessing, replaying the past, or focusing on the worst-case scenarios. Just as one train of thought settles down, I launch another.

Bing, bing, bing...

This thought crashes and bumps around unpredictably, while I play the game of trying to gain some control by continuing the cycle of planning, worrying, obsessing... you get the idea. Each part of the cycle is like the buttons on the side of the pinball machine. Feverishly, I push the buttons working to keep the ball in the maze. Pushing those buttons creates the illusion of control, but in reality, it just perpetuates the chaos.

I pray for peace, while I'm still actively keeping anxious thoughts bumping all around. I just keep launching more of my focus into the jumble.

Plan, worry, obsess...

The "noise" between my ears keeps me from peace.

We sure can get ourselves worked up when we focus on our struggles and circumstances. God offers us perfect peace, yet there are obstacles, distractions, and deep wounds. There are seasons of life when perfect peace seems impossible. When we're just trying to keep fighting through the chaos.

But what if we choose to stop fighting?

Let's look again at today's key verse -

"You keep him in perfect peace whose mind is stayed on you because he trusts you." Isaiah 26:3

God's perfect peace isn't the result of God removing the hardships from our lives. He isn't promising a perfect life.

What does it look like to have a mind "stayed" on the Lord?

It means **we submit to the God who is in control and relinquish our illusion of control**. Keeping our mind on the Lord means we choose to step back. We refuse to keep our anxious thoughts circulating in the clutter of our minds.

Instead, we let our minds *rest* as we focus on the character of God. He is righteous and just. He is loving and compassionate. He is the God of peace, not disorder (1 Corinthians 14:33).

We must recognize that our worries don't change His will. But when we focus on him, he changes our thoughts from chaos to peace.

Dear Heavenly Father,
I praise you for being the God
of peace. You know the mess in my anxious
mind. I have been trying hard to fix it on
my own, making me a slave to the illusion
of control. Today, I commit to focusing on
your character. I choose to keep my mind
stayed on you. I trust you, Father.
In Jesus' Name, Amen

Finding Your Footing

What are the thoughts that continue to "bounce" around in your mind? In what ways are your thoughts keeping you from perfect peace?

____

____

____

____

____

Look up 2 Thessalonians 3:16. Write this out as a prayer for yourself and your circumstances.

____

____

____

____

____

Extra Notes

When the Storm Rages

"'Lord, save me.' Jesus immediately reached out his hand and took hold of him" Matthew 14:30b - 31a

The spray of the water hit Peter in the face as he strained against the oar. It had been a long day, and it looked like the night ahead wouldn't bring much rest. The grunts of effort from the other men in the boat were lost in the wind. The unpredictable waves tossed their boat even farther off course. Each of the disciples focused on surviving the storm.

Suddenly, the sound of yelling grabbed Peter's attention. He stood looking in the direction his fellow disciples were pointing.

"It's a ghost!" Peter finally made out what he was hearing. His heart jumped into his throat.

Water surrounded a ghostly silhouette. The figure's feet were visible atop the water and the waves seemed to only lift the body higher.

"Take courage!" A familiar voice called out from the waves. "It is I. Don't be afraid."

Peter knew the voice of his teacher and friend Jesus. But his eyes couldn't make sense of what he saw.

"And Peter answered him, 'Lord, if it is you, command me to come to you on the water.'

He said, 'Come.'

So Peter got out of the boat and walked on the water and came to Jesus. But when he saw the wind, he was afraid, and beginning to sink he cried out, 'Lord, save me.'

"Jesus immediately reached out his hand and took hold of him, saying to him, "O you of little faith, why did you doubt?"' Matthew 14:28-31

You may recognize this story. (The first few paragraphs are just a picture in my head of the details that may have led up to Peter walking on the water. Read Matthew 14:22-27 for the details we know about the situation.)

I've heard sermons and read several commentaries about Peter in this story. Some praise him for stepping out of the boat, some chide him for his lack of faith to stay afloat. Many point out Peter's focus was on the waves and wind, instead of on Jesus. All of these are great points!

However, for today, let's turn our attention to what we learn about Jesus in Matthew 14:22-33.

First, we see evidence that **Jesus comes to us during the storm**. It didn't matter to Jesus that the boat was far from shore, or that there were considerable waves (v. 24).

Jesus can do the same thing for us. **When the storms of life seem bigger than our ability to row, our savior shows up walking on the waves.**

Another lesson we can learn in this passage is that **Jesus rescues us when we fall**. We read about Peter's literal step of faith onto the waves. When his faith faltered, Peter called out, *"Lord, save me!"* (v. 30). The next phrase of this passage makes me tear up.

Matthew tells us *"Immediately Jesus reached out his hand and took hold of him"* (v. 31). **Immediately!** Jesus didn't let Peter sink up to his eyeballs before he rescued him. He didn't withhold his hand. No, *immediately* after Peter cried out, Jesus reached out.

This is the same Jesus that rescued us from eternity apart from him, simply because we call on his name (Romans 10:13).

Jesus challenged Peter's doubt after having stepped onto the water in faith. But these earnest words from Jesus were only spoken after he had taken hold of Peter.

Choosing faith is a process. Sometimes we falter or even fall, just as Peter did.

Praise the Lord that we have a Savior who comes to us in the storms of life and rescues us when we call on him.

Dear Heavenly Father,
Thank you for sending Jesus to
show us more of who you are.
Jesus was the perfect example of how to
live and he saved us from the consequences
of our sins. Thank you that you show up for
me in hard times, as Jesus did for Peter.
I will call out to you when I am afraid.
Rescue me from drowning in doubts.
In Jesus' Name, Amen

Finding Your Footing

Read all of Matthew 14:22-33. What was the disciples' response after Jesus and Peter climbed into the boat (v. 33)? How has God shown up in your storms?

Read Romans 10:9-13. How does this passage relate to Peter's experience on the water? Is this passage in Romans referring to a physical rescue?

Extra Notes

When You Need a Trustworthy Friend

"The Lord is a stronghold for the oppressed, a stronghold in times of trouble. And those who know your name put their trust in you, for you, O Lord, have not forsaken those who seek you." Psalm 9:9-10

Do you have a trustworthy friend? One that you know you can count on? A friend that will show up when you need them?

I am blessed to have a few friends like this. When I tell them something in confidence, I know they will not betray that confidence. When I need something, I trust they will jump in to help. When I'm hurting, I know they will show up by my side.

I trust them because I *know* each one very well. There is a record of past behavior that allows me to know their character. I have spent time with them and built a relationship with them over countless cups of coffee, and endless conversations.

It's harder for me to have the same kind of trust in someone I don't know. I am not likely to spill my soul to someone I just met or ask them for help. I don't expect much from a passing acquaintance. Without a relationship, I have no reason to trust that they care for me.

I pray you have at least one trustworthy friend. But even if you haven't found that kind of friendship yet, I have good news for you. The Lord is even more trustworthy than our very best friend! **He is worthy of our deepest level of trust.**

Today's verses tell us that the Lord is worthy of trust because of who he is. He is a stronghold. A place of security. He will not abandon anyone who seeks him.

"Those who know your name put their trust in you" Psalm 9:10.

If we commit to seeking him and learning as much as we can about the character of God, we will *know* that we can trust him. Even if we are disappointed by the circumstances in our lives, we will be certain that the Lord himself will not leave us or forsake us (Deuteronomy 31:8).

To know the Lord is to trust him. So, in seasons when we struggle to *trust him*, we must be willing to diligently *seek him*.

Just as with any relationship, we get to know God better by spending time with him. We read his Word to learn about who he is. We understand more of his character by looking at what he has done – both in his word and all around us. We talk to him and share our fears and failures with him. We listen to the Holy Spirit as he teaches us to discern God's best for our lives.

All of this sounds so simple. And in a way it is – we seek him so that we know him better. And when

we know the Lord, we can trust him.

But the Lord God is more complex than we will ever comprehend. His ways are not our ways. His thoughts are not our thoughts (Isaiah 55:8). We will experience things on this earth that shake our view of who we *thought* God was.

That is where our **faith must bridge the gap between what we know about our Heavenly Father, and what we cannot yet understand.** We may not understand the pain he allows, but as we seek him, we will find he *never leaves us*. He is our safe place. We can trust him because we know him.

Dear Heavenly Father,
Thank you for being the most
trustworthy friend. I long to know you
deeper. When trouble comes, I will trust you.
Show me how to know you better.
In Jesus' Name, Amen

Finding Your Footing

Read Proverbs 3:5-6. In what ways are you tempted to *lean on your own understanding?*

What is one thing God has done to demonstrate that he is trustworthy? Think of examples from your own life, and the lives of others.

Extra Notes

When You Long for Compassion

I flopped onto my twin daybed, with a dramatic sigh, tears wetting my mint green comforter. In all my 17 years of life, I had never felt so overwhelmed. Hurt feelings, homework, and hard decisions all weighed on my young shoulders.

Suddenly, I heard the front door open. I froze.

Oh no! Now I'm really in trouble. My mind raced trying to think of an excuse for why I was home in the middle of the school day.

I knew my mom was out for the day, but I didn't expect my dad to come home in the middle of the day! I thought about hiding.

"Hey!" My dad called out from just inside the front door.

He must have seen my car in the driveway. Time to face the music.

"I'm in here," I answered, feeling defeated.

Seconds later my dad stood in the doorway.

"You alright?" He asked.

I considered making up some physical ailment as an excuse for skipping school that day. But I didn't.

Over the next several minutes I poured my heart out. Despite my decision to be honest, my voice held all the attitude of a teenager who knew she was about to be grounded.

Instead of delivering a lecture, my dad stayed quiet. He made his way to my side and sat on the edge of the bed while he listened.

When I finally wrapped up my rant, my father validated my feelings and gave me a short pep talk. To my surprise, he didn't say a word about me skipping school. I wondered if I would hear about my punishment later when he discussed the situation with my mom. But it was never spoken of again.

My dad showed me compassion that afternoon. More than empathy. He chose not to add to my stress with a lecture. He genuinely wanted to help me feel heard and to relieve some of my overwhelming self-doubts.

I recognize the blessing of having a father who demonstrated mercy and compassion to me. I've learned that unfortunately, many people did not grow up with a father who reflected God's love to them.

But **praise the Lord, that HE is a compassionate father. He loves us perfectly.**

I often think of compassion as simply empathy or even pity. But compassion is more than that. **Compassion includes the desire to lessen another's pain. A desire to help.**

Whether we are 17 or 117 we will experience times when we are overwhelmed by the climb ahead. There will be moments when we feel as if we can't take another step. But God is a compassionate father.

He desires to alleviate our heartache. **When our hearts are broken, his heart longs to heal us.**

We can trust God's character. We can choose faith that he "shows compassion to those who fear him" (Psalm 103:13).

When we recognize that God is the Lord of everything, we can experience his compassion. He is not cruel. God doesn't allow painful circumstances simply to watch us suffer. He longs to ease our suffering.

May we lean into his arms of compassion and allow him to carry us on this difficult journey.

Dear Heavenly Father,
Thank you for being a
compassionate father.
You long to heal my broken heart.
Allow me to recognize your compassion
today. Help me to become more aware of
how you are working on my behalf.
In Jesus' Name, Amen

Finding Your Footing

Read all of Psalm 103. List any other characteristics of God mentioned in this chapter.

Look up 1 Peter 5:6-7. What does this passage say we should do to our cares/anxieties? Is this a passive process on our part? Or does it require action?

Extra Notes

When God Feels Distant

"How long, O Lord? Will you forget me forever? How long will you hide your face from me? How long must I take counsel in my soul and have sorrow in my heart all the day? How long shall my enemy be exalted over me?" Psalm 13:1-2
"But I have trusted in your steadfast love; my heart shall rejoice in your salvation. I will sing to the Lord, because he has dealt bountifully with me."
Psalm 13:5-6

I love the Psalms. I often find words to describe my feelings in the songs written thousands of years ago. In Psalm 13, David cries out to God in a way that most of us can probably relate to.

David prays so honestly. He is not seeing God move. He feels forgotten by the Lord. He feels alone in his sorrow.

Have you ever been in that space? I know I have. When life seems to be running hard in a direction that takes me farther away from where I want to be. When the hurt seems crushing. When I can't see a way out of my hardships. When I wonder if God is even paying any attention.

I am so grateful that we see people in the Bible being honest with God. Our feelings are not unimportant to the Lord. Praise our compassionate Heavenly Father that we don't need to filter our feelings when we pray.

But…

This one word shows up in Psalm 13:5, and changes everything. After spending four verses pouring out his raw and honest feelings, David says,

*"**But** I have trusted in your steadfast love; my heart shall rejoice in your salvation."* Psalm 13:5 (Emphasis mine.)

It seems David contradicts himself in this Psalm. He accuses God of forgetting him (v. 1) and then says he trusts God's unfailing love (v. 5) David tells God he is drowning in sorrow (v. 2) and then says his heart rejoices in the Lord's salvation (v. 5).

It may seem odd until we take a closer look. In verses 1-4, David's cry is focused on his struggles, **but** verses 5-6 David shifts his focus to his savior.

David couldn't *see* God's love, **but** he trusted it. He didn't *feel* joyful, **but** he chose to rejoice in the one who would bring his salvation. David *felt* defeated, **but** he chose to sing to the Lord who is worthy. He didn't *feel* God's goodness in the moment, **but** he knew that God had been good to him.

It's okay to ask God the hard questions. It's okay to go to him in our hurt and disappointment. There will be moments, even seasons, that we feel far from God, just as David did when he wrote Psalm 13.

***But* let us lift our eyes from our struggles to our savior.** We can choose to rejoice in the one who sacrificed his life for our salvation. We can choose to sing, simply because he is worthy. We can call to mind times that God has been good to us in the past.

We can hold both sorrow and celebration because of our faith in who God is.

Our emotions are *real* and they *matter* to our Lord. We don't need to pretend when we go to him in prayer. In fact, when we take those emotions to God in true lament, **he strengthens our faith and brings us deep joy in who he is and what he has done for us.**

Dear Heavenly Father,
*Life is hard, **but** you are good.*
I choose to set my eyes on you, my savior,
instead of on my struggles. Thank you for
listening to my pain-filled prayers. Help
me to see the ways you have "dealt
bountifully with me." (Psalm 13:6)
In Jesus' Name, Amen

Finding Your Footing

Write about a time when the Lord felt distant. How can you relate to how David was feeling in Psalm 13:1-4?

____

____

____

____

Write out this short six-verse chapter, personalizing it to be your prayer to God in a time of sorrow.

____

____

____

____

____

Extra Notes

When the Mountain Doesn't Move

Week Four

When You're Not Strong Enough

"He gives power to the faint, and to him who has no might he increases strength." Isaiah 40:29

Music played as family and friends shuffled out of the worship center. Many were still wiping their tears. Most were silent.

Because Faith Isabella died less than an hour after she was born, her memorial service was our only chance to introduce our daughter to those we loved. It was precious and heartbreaking all at once.

A friend wrapped me in a hug and whispered in my ear, "You're so strong."

"It's not me," I said immediately. "I'm not strong enough."

Versions of this conversation played out over and over that evening, and in the weeks that followed.

I suppose it looked like strength to others when they saw me out of the house. But I knew the truth.

People like to say, "God will never give you more than you can handle." Well, I'm here to tell you that is unbiblical and far from the truth! Many of God's people in scripture were given more than they could handle.

God *will* allow more than we can handle. But he will also give us unexplainable strength to survive the unsurvivable.

Through the loss of Faith Isabella and bouts of debilitating depression, there have been more days than I care to admit when I couldn't bear to get out of bed. If I had to rely on my own strength, I may still be there today. But, only through God's strength and mercy, I am here writing to you. It is certainly *not* because I am strong enough.

When we experience the worst of this life, it can rob us of our resilience. But God can give us his *unending* power.

So how do we access God's abundant strength?

There is no special code, or secret passage to receive the treasure of God's strength in our weakest moments. But here are a few prerequisites we see in scripture.

- **We must be weak or weary** (Isaiah 40:29). Raise your hand if you have this one down. I know I do!

- **We must trust in him to give us the strength we need** (Psalm 28:7-8). Do you believe that he can give you the strength you need for this moment? Don't rush ahead to tomorrow. His strength will be available when you get there. God will give you what you need for today (Matthew 6:34).

- **We must receive it** (2 Corinthians 12:9). Is there a part of you that is still trying to climb this mountain alone? It takes sincere humility to admit that we need God to help us, or even carry us on this journey.

Sometimes you may not even realize the strength God is providing for you until the moment has passed.

I often look back and wonder how I had the strength to survive parts of this journey... then I remember - *It wasn't me. I am not strong enough.*

Dear Heavenly Father,
"O my Strength,
I will watch for you,
for you, O God, are my fortress." (Psalm
59:9). Lord, I admit that I can't do this
alone. I am not strong enough. I trust you
to provide me with your strength to carry
me through each moment.
In Jesus' Name, Amen

Finding Your Footing

Have you experienced God carrying you through a specific circumstance in the past? If not, have you witnessed this in someone else's life? Write down a few sentences or bullet points about that experience.

____

____

____

____

Read Psalms 119:28. Then choose to be strengthened by God's word. Use a search engine or your bible app to look up scripture about God's strength. Choose 2-3 verses to write out as reminders that you can trust in the strength of the Lord.

____

____

____

____

Extra Notes

When Belief Wavers

"Immediately the father of the child cried out and said, 'I believe; help my unbelief!'" Mark 9:24

"Hey Buster," I said softly as I unbuckled my sleepy toddler's car seat. His eyelids fluttered open.

I smiled at his groggy expression and whispered, "Guess what?" He sat up excitedly, wriggling his shoulders free of the unbuckled straps.

"What?" He whispered back, looking around.

"We're on a boat!" I pulled him out of the car and onto my hip. We stood on the open deck of a car ferry headed across Lake Champlain. We were in the middle of our first family road trip, and we thought this boat-ride would be one of the highlights for our little guy.

I looked at his face, expecting to see wonder and awe. Instead, he furrowed his brow and looked around.

"No," he said matter-of-factly, shaking his head. "Dis no boat."

My husband and I spent the entire ferry ride trying to prove to our toddler that he was, in fact, riding on a boat. We pointed out the water all around us, the land getting farther away, and the wake behind us. We never did manage to convince him.

To his little mind, a boat looked like the toy boat he played with in the bathtub. Boats had sails, and portholes, and surely cars did not go on boats! He refused to believe what we *knew* to be true.

I will admit that I fall into the same disbelief with my Heavenly Father.

Sometimes, in the middle of difficult circumstances, I look around and don't see the evidence I expect. When there is loss, I struggle to see evidence of God's goodness. When I feel despair, I seem to be blinded to hope. When I can't see the path ahead, I start to doubt his plans.

Sure, I believe that God is real. He created everything. He sent his son to save us from eternity without him. I believe His word is true. But somehow in day-to-day life, unbelief seeps into the crevices of my mind. It squeezes into the spaces of hopelessness and uncertainty.

I want to believe.
I believe... mostly.
I believe as much as I am capable of believing.
I believe that with God all things are possible... But I should probably figure it out myself, just in case.

My thoughts circle in these patterns of unbelief. That is when, no matter what God's word says, I'm like my toddler son, furrowing my brow and exclaiming, "Dis no boat!"

Mark 9:22-24 tells of a desperate father who also battled unbelief. He came to Jesus to plead on behalf of his son.

"'But if you can do anything, have compassion on us and help us.' And Jesus said to him, ''If you can'! All things are possible for one who believes.' Immediately the father of the child cried out and said, 'I believe; help my unbelief!'" Mark 9:22-24

This father likely struggled to find hope that his son could be saved. When he heard of this teacher and his disciples who were healing people, he went to them. Believing (at least as much as he dared to believe) that Jesus's disciples could help. However, they couldn't. So, when he pleaded with Jesus for help, his belief was understandably wavering.

When we find ourselves in a place of wavering belief, we can *ask* God to help us overcome our unbelief, just as the father did in Mark 9:24. Instead of feeling defeated by his doubts, this father asks Jesus to help him overcome his unbelief. He didn't allow his wavering belief to be the end of the story.

We can simply come to Jesus with all the belief we are able to muster, and humbly ask him for help. **We can ask our Savior to capture any residual unbelief in our souls and transform it into belief.**

Our Savior is willing to help us when our belief wavers. We need only ask.

Dear Heavenly Father,
I confess that circumstances
cause my belief to waver.
I am unsure of your plan. Help my unbelief.
Infuse my heart with the courage to believe
what I cannot today.
In Jesus' Name, Amen

Finding Your Footing

Read the full story of today's key verse in Mark 9:14-27.
How can you relate to how the father in this story?
What unbelief are you holding on to?

____

____

____

____

Write out a simple prayer to God expressing your
desire to believe and asking him to help your unbelief.

____

____

____

____

____

Extra Notes

When You Face the Flames

"If we are thrown into the blazing furnace, the God we serve is able to deliver us from it, and he will deliver us from Your Majesty's hand. But even if he does not, we want you to know, Your Majesty, that we will not serve your gods or worship the image of gold you have set up." Daniel 3:17-18 NIV

When we face an unmoving mountain, we have a choice. We can choose to turn toward God, or away from him. The story of Shadrach, Meshach, and Abednego is a powerful account of three men who refused to turn away from God.

The mountain these three men faced was a ninety-foot-tall golden statue. They were required to worship the statue by order of the king himself. But they refused. They knew this statue was not the living God. And they knew that God had commanded his people not to worship any other god (Ex. 20:3).

When the king threatened the men with death by fiery furnace, they *still* refused to obey the king's order. Their response is our key passage today. Together Shadrach, Meshach, and Abednego turned squarely *toward* the Lord. The men knew that God was capable of rescuing them, but they showed complete obedience to God.

They spoke two simple, yet powerful, words.

"Even if..."

These words speak volumes about Shadrach, Meshach, and Abednego's faith. They chose to follow God, *even if* they lost their lives for it. *Even if* the One who was able to rescue them, chose not to. *Even if* it hurt.

We read in scripture that God does not save them from going into the fiery furnace. The fire was so hot that the guards who delivered them died from experiencing the heat themselves. Yet, miraculously, Shadrach, Meshach, and Abednego all survived the unsurvivable.

Imagine the moment the three men were tossed into the fire. Their hearts and minds were in the middle of the *"even if."* Knowing God could keep them safe, somehow. While, at the same time, knowing he might not.

One moment they may have felt unsure of God's plan, and the next they were walking through the flames with a fourth man leading them.

Who provided supernatural protection for the brave men inside the flames? God did! (Remember he never leaves us!)

You and I know what it's like to face the fire. We know God could keep us from hurt. We know he could bring miraculous healing. We know he is able to repair what's broken. We know he could step in before a heart-shattering tragedy occurs.

But what if he doesn't?

Could you and I stand as Shadrach, Meshach, and Abednego did and say, *"Even if the worst happens, I will not turn away from God"*? Or perhaps even more challenging, *"Even though the worst has happened, I will turn toward God"*?

One last challenging thought for today. Could we be bowing to the idol of comfort? Could we be turning away from God in an effort to avoid a painful circumstance?

Turning toward God may mean sacrificing our comfort. It may mean we find ourselves facing the fire.

We know that our God can do all things. But will we choose to turn toward him, even if he doesn't keep us from the flames of hardship?

Dear Heavenly Father,
Thank you for never leaving me,
even in the midst of suffering.
I choose to turn toward you even if
circumstances are not what I want. Lord,
I trust your plan, even if it hurts.
In Jesus' Name, Amen

Finding Your Footing

Read Shadrach, Meshach, and Abednego's full story in Daniel 3. Write down anything that stands out to you about the faith of these three men.

____

____

____

____

Will you choose to turn toward God even when facing hardship? Write out an "even if" prayer to him.

A note from Carrie: Dear friend, if you find yourself in the middle of the furnace as you read this, I pray God will give you strength and comfort as you work through this difficult "assignment."

____

____

____

____

Extra Notes

When the Enemy Attacks

Each time I read today's key verse I picture a circus act performance.

A woman in a nearly blinding sequin outfit walks across the stage without ever turning her smiling face from the crowd. Intense music fills the air. As she nears stage right, the crowd sees a large upright circle roll into place. Suddenly the stage goes dark, but the music continues to build.

A single flame appears in the darkness. The flame spreads to a nearby object. The spotlight fades in on a man holding a bow in one hand and a flaming arrow in the other. The audience gasps in realization as they spot the sparkly woman, now attached to the large circle. *She is the target!*

The man notches the flaming arrow onto the string of his bow. The sparkling lady is still smiling.

Then, just as the man pulls the arrow back, the woman holds up a giant life-sized shield. The tension deflates and the show ends abruptly.

I suppose the picture in my mind is not an act worth paying to see. After all, the shield protects the woman from all danger. It's not a very entertaining act... unless you simply have an overwhelming love for sequins.

I, for one, cannot pull off sequins. Yet I still find myself the target of flaming arrows. Not from a man on stage, but from the enemy of my soul.

Satan seeks to steal, kill, and destroy (John 10:10). *He wants to steal our faith, kill our hope, and destroy our future.*

Satan doesn't have control over our circumstances. Only God has that power. Yet, Satan loves to see us struggle because when we struggle, we are vulnerable. That's when we are tempted to believe the lies of the enemy. He shoots his flaming arrows toward our weary hearts.

- » *God must not love you.*
- » *God doesn't want the best for you, if he did, he surely wouldn't have allowed this.*
- » *Didn't God say you could move mountains? So why are you stuck climbing this one?*
- » *Are you SURE you can trust God's word?*

Each arrow may seem reasonable in times of hardship. But none of these attacks are harmless.

Thankfully we have a shield... just like the sparkly lady! When we take up our shield of faith, we extinguish the flames. The arrows may still fly toward us, but they won't hit their mark. We are safe from their flames.

So how do we take up our shield of faith?

We simply *choose faith* that God is who he says he is, and he will do what he says he will do.

Our heavenly father loves us and wants the best for us. We don't have to have everything figured out. We don't have to know how this hardship fits into his plan. We don't have to follow the evil one as he tries to lead us astray with overwhelming doubts and fears.

We have a defense that keeps us safe from our enemy. All we have to do is choose to pick up our shield of faith.

Dear Heavenly Father,
I trust you, even when
I don't understand the reason behind my
suffering. You alone are in control.
Today, I choose to take up my shield of faith
to extinguish any temptations that lead me
away from you.
In Jesus' Name, Amen

Finding Your Footing

Read about the full armor of God in Ephesians 6:10-17. What are the other pieces of armor that protect us from the evil one?

____

____

____

____

Draw a shield. (Don't worry, there are no points for artistic ability.) On your shield write three bible verses that will encourage your heart to choose faith in times you feel attacked by the enemy.

Extra Notes

When You Can't Find
the Words to Pray

"Likewise the Spirit helps us in our weakness. For we do not know what to pray for as we ought, but the Spirit himself intercedes for us with groanings too deep for words." Romans 8:26

Tears made my phone screen slip against my cheek.

"My heart is just broken, Mom." I sobbed.

"I know sweetheart." My mother said softly. "Have you prayed about this?"

I fought the urge to roll my eyes, sure that my mom would somehow see through the cell phone.

"No." I responded flatly. "I'm so hurt, I don't even know where to start. What do I even pray for?"

"Well, we know from God's word that the Holy Spirit intercedes for us even when we can't find the words. You don't have to know what to say."

My mom prayed for me and quickly wrapped up our phone call.

I sat confused, still holding my phone. I expected to

rant to my mom for another hour or so. I wanted to let her know each detail about the mess I was caught in. I wanted to tell her how I had been wronged, disappointed, and how God didn't stop any of it! But instead, my mom seemed to rush me off the phone.

After several minutes of self pity, I put my phone to use again and typed "Holy Spirit intercedes for us" into the search engine. A few taps later, I read -

"Likewise the Spirit helps us in our weakness. For we do not know what to pray for as we ought, but the Spirit himself intercedes for us with groanings too deep for words." Romans 8:26

Suddenly I realized that my mother, who deeply loves God's word, was right (as she usually is). What she wanted for me, was what God wanted for me. To come to Him.

When something terrible occurs, it can be hard to know how to pray. The worst has happened. We are hurt. Our hearts are broken. What is there to say to the Lord?

Sometimes we immediately want to rant to our besties (or moms), and other times we want to hide under the covers hoping the hurt will pass. Or we may be tempted to find temporary comfort in our usual coping mechanisms (shopping, snacking, sipping, scrolling... etc).

But what if we could build a habit of going to God first? This doesn't mean we don't share our struggles with those we love. It simply means we trust the Holy Spirit to help, even when we can't find the words to pray.

It's easy to think of prayer as just words. But our key verse today is evidence that **prayer is more than just syllables and sentences.** It says that the Holy Spirit communicates to the Father for us with "groanings too deep for words."

We can cry out to the Lord with our own groaning. With our sobs. Tears can be our prayers. We can tell God how hurt we are, with or without words.

I've often pictured myself crawling up onto the lap of my Heavenly Father like a toddler and crying into his shoulder. **There is comfort in his arms** (Psalm 16:1). **Refuge in the shadow of his wings** (Psalm 91:4). **Rest in the peace of his presence** (Psalm 4:8).

God doesn't want us to wait to come to him until we have our feelings all sorted out. He doesn't need, nor does he desire, a perfected prayer with flowery words or well thought out phrases.

The Lord simply wants us to come to him, even when we can't find the words to pray.

Dear Heavenly Father,
I don't always know what to say
when my heart is broken.
Thank you for providing your Holy Spirit to
intercede on my behalf. Help me to come to
you when I am hurting.
In Jesus' Name, Amen

Finding Your Footing

Read Matthew 14:30. Write out the three words Peter cried out to Jesus. (Remember we read the context of Peter's words last week) Have you ever prayed a similar prayer?

Imagine your compassionate and loving Heavenly Father is physically and visibly present in the room with you right now. How would you respond?

Extra Notes

When the Mountain Doesn't Move

Week Five

When the View is Cloudy

We walked up the steep path. I was trying my best not to pant too loudly.

"Why did I think this was going to be easier?" I said between breaths.

My husband laughed. "I'm glad I'm not the only one struggling."

Our family was visiting Clingmans Dome in North Carolina – the highest point in the Great Smoky Mountains.

When we left the parking area, we could see mountains for miles, even through the "smokiness" the area is known for. However, as we worked our way up the paved path we seemed to be in the middle of a cloud.

At the very peak of the path, we knew there was an observation tower. But when we came upon the structure, we could barely see the top of it. It was almost completely hidden behind the fog.

"There sure isn't much to observe from this 'observation tower'" I said through winded laughter.

When we reached the top of the tower, it was as if we were surrounded by a white blanket. We had read that on a clear day, you could see for 100 miles from the tower. But instead of sweeping mountain views, all we could see through our squinted eyes was white.

I held my phone up in camera mode, trying to decide the best way to capture the view... or lack of view.

"Here Mom!" My son called. He pointed to a plaque on the wall of the tower. "You can just take a close-up of this!"

I walked closer and zoomed in on the sign he pointed to. It was a wide-angle photograph of the landscape, with text labeling the names of the mountain peaks presumably visible from the tower.

I had a hard time believing the beauty in the picture was out there because my eyes saw only fog. *Was this really even the place we meant to end up? Was the climb even worth it?*

I've often thought about this experience and how it relates to life on this earth.

Sometimes we reach the top of the mountain, and we can see the beauty of what God has done all around us. We receive answers to our questions. We see the beauty he has
created from the ashes of disappointment.

Other times, we finish the hard climb and *can't* see past where our feet stand. Sometimes we don't get to know the purpose of our pain. We don't have a view of all the beauty that God is creating on this side of eternity. The view from the top doesn't always seem worth the climb.

Often our view after a difficult climb is clouded by the temporary circumstances we can't seem to escape from.

How do we handle that type of disappointment? Do we turn away from the God that carried us this far? Do we refuse to believe that there could be more to the story than we can see?

Or do we choose faith that God's purposes are still good, even when our vision is clouded by the painful present?

One day, we will see God's masterpiece he is creating with the intertwining threads of our lives. The panoramic view from a perspective that is hidden from us today. Because on that day we won't see only what is temporary, we will see the eternal masterpiece he has created. **Oh, how glorious that sight will be!**

Dear Heavenly Father,
Thank you that there is more to
my story than this moment.
Teach me how to live with an eternal
perspective so that I can endure hardship
with hope. Help me to trust that you are
creating beauty where all I see is ash.
In Jesus' Name, Amen

Finding Your Footing

Paul (the author of our key verse today) writes about some of the trouble he had encountered in 2 Corinthians 6:3-10. Read this passage and list the ways Paul had suffered. How does Paul's perspective on his "light momentary affliction" change your perspective on your own troubles?

____

____

____

____

Read Matthew 16:21-28. What is Jesus's response to Peter? How does Peter show that he is focused only on what is seen?

____

____

____

____

Extra Notes

When Drought Comes

"Blessed is the man who trusts in the Lord, whose trust is the Lord. He is like a tree planted by water, that sends out its roots by the stream, and does not fear when heat comes, for its leaves remain green, and is not anxious in the year of drought, for it does not cease to bear fruit." Jeremiah 17:7-8

Fall is a beautiful time of year in my home state of Michigan. It's a time filled with colorful leaves, sweaters, and fall traditions. One of our favorite fall traditions is going apple picking.

One fall we excitedly made our way to our favorite orchard. At this particular farm, you get a wagon ride from the barn to the endless rows of apple trees.

All three of us were excited about picking apples! But as we climbed off the wagon my husband noticed something odd.
"Uh... where are all the apples?" He asked.

"On the trees, silly!" Our five-year-old declared.

I looked at the bare trees and shrugged. "Maybe these ones have already been picked?"

We wandered into the thick of the orchard and searched several rows of trees. But all we found were bare branches.

Confused, we walked back toward where the wagon dropped us off. That's when we noticed the crowd.

"What are they doing?" I asked no one in particular. Just then the crowd cleared enough for me to spot a large wooden crate.

"I think they are picking apples!" My husband said. Sure enough, people were grabbing apples from the large crate.

After asking around we learned that the dry, hot summer had all but ruined the local apple crop that season. We couldn't be sure that the crate of apples was even from Michigan. I tried to have a good attitude. I knew the orchard was simply doing their best to stay afloat during a hard year. But honestly, it felt like a wasted trip. We may as well have gone to the grocery store to "pick" our apples!

When the heat comes and the rain doesn't, the fruit crop typically suffers.

Jeremiah 17:7-8 tells us that trusting in the Lord will keep us fruitful even in times of drought. How can this be? How can seasons of hardship produce anything good?

It can seem like our seasons of suffering are just wasted. But **nothing is wasted in the hands of the Lord.**

When we have faith in the Lord, we are like a tree planted by the water (v. 7).

When drought comes the roots of trees dig deeper into the soil in search of water. As a result, the tree grows a stronger root system and will not be easily moved by storms. A tree planted by the water *always* finds nourishment, no matter what the weather.

Praise the Lord, he sent us the living water in the person of Jesus Christ (John 4:10)! **As we sit in the suffering of this season, we can dig our roots deep into our faith and we will find our eternal source of nourishment.**

We don't have to fake it. We don't have to look elsewhere for comfort or for momentary satiation. We can have confidence that our needs will be met, and we will thrive again.

The fruit that God grows as we choose to trust him is the fruit of *purpose.* **We may not understand why we are in this season of suffering, but we can be sure it will not be wasted.**

God will bring fruit. He will bring purpose. He will continue to grow our roots strong, even in the middle of the drought.

Dear Heavenly Father,
Thank you for sustaining me
through this difficult season.
This suffering is nothing I would have
chosen, but I don't want it to be wasted.
Help me to root myself in you so that you
can produce purpose from this pain.
In Jesus' Name, Amen

Finding Your Footing

Read Genesis 41:46-52. What name did Joseph give his second son? Why does he choose this name? Can you see any fruit from your "land of affliction" yet? If not, it's okay... remember God will not waste even this.

____

____

____

____

Read Jeremiah 17:5-8. Write down the differences between the one who trusts in man, versus the one who trusts in the Lord.

____

____

____

____

____

Extra Notes

When Suffering Seems Senseless

"Then Job answered the Lord and said: 'I know that you can do all things, and that no purpose of yours can be thwarted. 'Who is this that hides counsel without knowledge?' Therefore, I have uttered what I did not understand, things too wonderful for me, which I did not know."
Job 42:1-3

After our infant daughter died, Job became my favorite book of the Bible. I would often sit in my most comfy chair, bible in hand, and cheer on "my pal" Job as he ranted about the unfairness of what God had put him through.

Job *knew* suffering. All of his children died, his wealth disappeared, his reputation was ruined, and his body was covered in painful sores. He questioned God's purpose for his pain (Job 9:17). He said he had no hope (Job 7:6). He even wished he had never been born (Job 10:18-20). Reading through Job you can see his anger build as he grieves the loss of all that he loved.

Job recognized God's sovereignty over all things. But he felt no peace in that knowledge. Instead, he felt that the God of the universe was cruel. Job feared what God had planned for his future.

"What he desires, that he does. For he will complete what he appoints for me, and many such things are in his mind. Therefore, I am terrified at his presence; when I consider, I am in dread of him." Job 23:13-15

This same fear of the future held me captive for a time. I was terrified of what was next. I knew that God was in control, but that brought anxiety that he would allow more pain in my future. In talking to others who have experienced loss or trauma, this feeling is not unique to me and my pal, Job.

Job was attacked from every angle by Satan himself. From our human perspective Job's feelings were certainly justified.

But then we read that *"the Lord answered Job out of the whirlwind"* (Job 38:1). When God showed up, Job saw the error of his heart. After chapters of ranting, Job answers God in very few words (Job 42:2-6).

Job experienced God's awesome presence in a way that made him immediately retract the words spoken in anger. Job humbled himself before God. He recognized that although he didn't understand God's plan, he knew that there was a purpose to it. "No purpose of yours can be thwarted." Job 42:2

The book of Job ends with God restoring Job's life. (However, no amount of wealth and future children took away the fact that Job had experienced great loss. Check out Job 42:10-11 to see evidence that Job didn't just "move on.")

However, something that is often missed is that Job didn't *wait* to choose faith in God's plans until after his life was restored. It wasn't the prosperity God provided that turned Job's heart around. It was the presence of God that changed everything.

God's presence isn't reserved for ancient times and people like Job. Scripture tells us *"The Lord is near to the brokenhearted and saves the crushed in spirit."* Psalm 34:18

The Lord is near to us *now*.

God has never shown up to me in a literal storm as he did for Job, but that's probably for the best... I'm not sure my heart (or my bladder) could handle that! However, he shows his presence to my shattered heart in precious moments hidden in seasons of pain.

There is a sacredness in our sorrow when the Lord draws near.

For Job, experiencing a moment in the midst of God's greatness transformed his heart. For us, the Lord promises his presence in the middle of our suffering.

Could God's presence be enough to turn our faith toward him? Could we choose to submit to the Lord's purposes for our present and our future?

Dear Heavenly Father,
You are sovereign Lord.
Forgive me for the times I have presumed
to know what is best. Your plans may not
always make sense to my earthly brain,
but I trust you are using them for heavenly
gain. Allow me to experience your presence
as you draw near.
In Jesus' Name, Amen

Finding Your Footing

Read some of the Lord's words to Job in Job 40:6-14. Does the Lord answer any of Job's questions? Does the Lord's response satisfy Job (see today's key verses)?

The Lord says he is near to the brokenhearted (Ps. 34:18). Write a list of five ways you have experienced his nearness in your season of suffering. (God can show his presence in something as simple as a text from a friend)

Extra Notes

When You Search for Value

"In this you rejoice, though now for a little while, if necessary, you have been grieved by various trials, so that the tested genuineness of your faith—more precious than gold that perishes though it is tested by fire—may be found to result in praise and glory and honor at the revelation of Jesus Christ." 1 Peter 1:6-7

For thousands of years gold has been used as a standard of value. It is thought that the ancient Egyptians were the first to mine for gold. Since that time, across millennia, cultures, and jurisdictions, gold has been considered precious.

As I type these words, one gram of gold is worth about $75. (For reference a gram of gold can fit on your fingertip!)

Gold holds value for several reasons. Here are just a few reasons why gold is considered valuable.

Gold is -
* A limited resource – there is only so much gold on the earth.
* Difficult to find and extract from the earth.
* Unique in its ability to be reshaped for different uses.

- Resistant to corrosion so it will never rust or tarnish.
- And, let's be honest, gold is beautiful!

Gold has been used as a symbol of status, a prize for excellence, a foundation for currency, and is the most sought-after precious metal for jewelry.

In today's key verses Peter writes that our genuine faith is worth *more* than gold. And how is our faith proved genuine? By the testing of our faith through trials.

The value isn't *past* the mountain that we commanded to move, it's *in* it.

Through the trials I have faced so far in this life, God has taught me that faith in him is a choice. And as I choose faith in our good God, I discover that the ground I once commanded to be thrown into the sea is not just an obstacle. I have seen the value in its soil. The good hidden beneath its steep rocks... ***The "golden good."***

After all, gold is not found when a mountain moves, it is found in the exploration of the mountain itself.

In our desperation, the value of trials is easy to miss. Often the purpose of our suffering takes time to show up. The full value may not be visible until seen through the light of eternity.

However, God's word is clear that there is golden good that we can collect on our mountains of hardship.

When we choose faith, we –
- Experience God's compassion and mercy (James 5:10)
- Are able to comfort others with the comfort we have received from the Lord (2 Corinthians 1:3-4)
- Desire even more time in God's presence (Psalm 42:1-2)
- Grow our roots of faith strong in him (Psalm 1:3)
- Find strength in God's word (Psalm 119:28)
- Discover God's power in our weaknesses (2 Corinthians 12:9)

But the golden good doesn't end there. **Our genuine faith in trials will be rewarded on the other side of this life** as well.

"Blessed is the man who remains steadfast under trial, for when he has stood the test he will receive the crown of life, which God has promised to those who love him."
James 1:12

Hang on, Dear One. It may not be obvious right now, but you *will* be rewarded for your faith in trials. And **the eternal reward for choosing faith will far outweigh the cost of the climb** (2 Corinthians 4:17).

Dear Heavenly Father,
You are a good God who can
bring something of value out of rocks.
I trust that there is value even in this
difficult time. Show me the golden good you
have for me on this mountain.
In Jesus' Name, Amen

Finding Your Footing

Look back at the list of the *golden good* we can experience when we choose faith. Look up at least 2 verses from the list. Can you relate to any of these "golden goods"?

____

____

____

____

Look up Romans 5:3-4 and James 1:2-4. What is similar about these passages? What would it look like for you to "count it all joy"?

____

____

____

____

____

Extra Notes

When We Choose Faith

"And we know that for those who love God all things work together for good, for those who are called according to his purpose." Romans 8:28

"If one more person quotes Romans 8:28 to me," I ranted to my sister, "I might just kick them in the shin!"

I flopped down on the couch and realized I was talking into my phone far louder than necessary. However, my big sister had no judgment. She simply joined in the rant with me. She always has my back. And I'm sure she packs a mean shin kick! (Don't worry, no shins were ever kicked... I'm all talk.)

Romans 8:28 was such a difficult verse for me to understand when I was in the depths of grief. (If you are in that place today, God sees you. I am proud of you for getting this far into today's devotion.)

I wrestled hard with God about what this verse meant. *How could he work the death of our baby girl for good?*

With time, I was able to read Romans 8:28 without my blood pressure rising. I even started to ask God to "help my unbelief" (Mark 9:24) concerning his promise to "work all things for the good" (Romans 8:28). The

Lord's answer to my prayer came from an unexpected place.

Each year our city hosts a large international art competition. Exhibits range from small portraits to large outdoor statues, and everything in between.

One type of art that kept drawing my attention was "recycled art." Recycled art transforms literal trash into works of art.

The artists use broken glass, ripped up newspapers, rusted auto parts, tarnished silverware, crushed water bottles... anything bound for the landfill, to create a thing of beauty. When you look closely you can see items that hold no appeal on their own.

I have never thought of any of these everyday items as attractive. But someone far more gifted than I, sees a way to create beauty out of things that have no beauty on their own.

Through these art pieces, God reminded me that **he is the original redemptive artist.** He creates beauty out of things that hold no beauty on their own.

God grows magnificent blossoms from dirt. He created the incredibly complex human body from dust. He brought water from a rock, beauty from ashes, and salvation from a cross.

He is the God who redeems all things.

My heart softened to the idea that even the worst pain in my life could be used to grow something of worth.

Something of beauty.

As we climb this mountain that God allowed to stay put, he is creating a masterpiece. A work of art that will glorify him.

The truth is, **God does not need our permission to use our stories for his glory. However, he invites us to be part of the beauty he is creating.**

He invites us to commit even the most broken parts of our lives to him. Because *nothing* is beyond his redemption.

Choose to step forward with me.

Choose to step onto the bridge of faith that connects what we see with what we know to be true. **Let's choose to believe that God is creating something beautiful from our time on the mountain he didn't move. Let's choose to be part of the masterpiece he is creating.**

Let's choose faith with each step!

Dear Heavenly Father,
I choose faith that you are good
and your plan for me is good.
I want to be part of the beauty you are
creating. Grant me the strength to continue
forward in faith.
In Jesus' Name, Amen

Finding Your Footing

Read aloud the verses you committed to reading in Week 2. What have these verses meant in your life over the past 20 days? (If you found this practice helpful, keep it up! Perhaps choose 2-3 new verses each month.)

____

____

____

____

Read Hebrews 11 again. (We read it on Day 1 as well.) The people mentioned in this chapter all choose to live "by faith." Write a sentence or two about your life as you step forward choosing to live by faith. Start with "By faith (your name),..."

____

____

____

____

Extra Notes

Connect with the Author

- Find more encouragement at
  www.ChoosingFaith23.com

- Keep up with the latest news from Choosing Faith
  23 by signing up to receive emails from CF23.

- Connect with Carrie online on Instagram
  @ChoosingFaith23

- Or on Facebook at
  www.facebook.com/choosingfaith23

- Email Carrie personally at
  Carrie@choosingfaith23.com

www.ingramcontent.com/pod-product-compliance
Lightning Source LLC
Chambersburg PA
CBHW071618150726
48000CB00004B/1782